The Wonder of
RACCOONS

To Mom, who put up with the clothesline capers, and to Dad, who caught the crayfish in Kellig Run, so long ago.
— Jeff Fair

For a free color catalog describing Gareth Stevens' list of high-quality books and multimedia programs, call 1-800-542-2595 (USA) or 1-800-461-9120 (Canada). Gareth Stevens Publishing's Fax: (414) 225-0377. See our catalog, too, on the World Wide Web: http://gsinc.com

Library of Congress Cataloging-in-Publication Data

Ritchie, Rita.
    The wonder of raccoons / by Rita Ritchie and Jeff Fair ; photographs by Alan and Sandy Carey ; illustrations by John F. McGee.
        p. cm. — (Animal wonders)
    "Based on . . . Raccoon magic for kids . . . by Jeff Fair"—T.p. verso.
    Includes index.
    Summary: Provides information about the physical characteristics, habits, and behavior of raccoons.
    ISBN 0-8368-1562-9 (lib. bdg.)
    1. Raccoons—Juvenile literature. [1. Raccoons.] I. Fair, Jeff. II. Carey, Alan, ill.
III. Carey, Sandy, ill. IV. McGee, John F., ill. V. Fair, Jeff. Raccoons. VI. Title. VII. Series.
QL737.C26R57   1996
599.74'443--dc20   96-5176

First published in North America in 1996 by
Gareth Stevens Publishing
1555 North RiverCenter Drive, Suite 201
Milwaukee, WI 53212 USA

This edition is based on the book *Raccoon Magic for Kids* © 1993 by Jeff Fair, first published in the United States in 1993 by NorthWord Press, Inc., Minocqua, Wisconsin, and published in a library edition by Gareth Stevens, Inc., in 1995. All photographs © 1993 by Alan and Sandy Carey, with illustrations by John F. McGee. Additional end matter © 1996 by Gareth Stevens, Inc.

Printed in the United States of America

1 2 3 4 5 6 7 8 9 99 98 97 96

CL
3/98   A547610

The Wonder of
RACCOONS

by Rita Ritchie and Jeff Fair
Photographs by Alan and Sandy Carey
Illustrations by John F. McGee

Gareth Stevens Publishing

MILWAUKEE

Raccoons live in the same places people live. They also prowl the woods and banks of streams. They investigate farms and fields. They even go into the backyards of homes.

Raccoons live in most of
North America. But they do
not like to live in deserts, high
mountains, or very cold places.

A raccoon
seems to
have a
mask on
its face.
Its bushy
tail has
rings.
Raccoon
fur is a
yellow-
gray color.

In spring, a mother raccoon finds a den high in a hollow tree. She has three or four babies, called kits, in the den each year.

At two months, the mother moves the kits from the tree den to a den near the ground. There, the kits start to discover the world. Raccoons like shiny objects because they look wet. A lot of foods they eat, such as snails and fish, are wet.

Raccoons are very smart. Once, some fishermen teased a raccoon by tying food to a fishing line. They kept pulling the food out of the raccoon's reach. But behind the fishermen's backs, other raccoons came into their camp. They opened the coolers and took *all* the food!

Raccoons are usually nocturnal, or active at night. But they *can* hunt in daylight. They have been known to come to cabins during the day to beg for food.

Raccoons use their front paws to grab and feel objects. They have five long toes on each foot. They walk on the soles of their feet just the way humans do.

It is unwise and dangerous to both the animal and people when a raccoon is taken from its natural home.

At about three months, the kits start following their mothers to look for food. But the kits don't go far from the den at first.

Soon, the kits go farther from the den. But some have to be carried in mother's mouth.

By end of summer, the young ones can find their own meals. Some move away, but most stay until the following spring. Then they may move 30-100 miles (50-160 kilometers) away.

A raccoon has more than one den. Raccoons live in trees, under rock ledges, and in burrows. Dens in the ground are warm in winter and cool in summer. Raccoons also live in hollow logs, junk piles, lumber stacks, barns, attics, sheds, chimneys, and old cars.

Raccoons eat plants and animals. They eat fruits, corn, grains, and grasses. They eat snails, slugs, toads, butterflies, eggs, worms, snakes, lizards, turtles, ducks, rabbits, and mice. In autumn, they eat acorns and other nuts.

Raccoons also hunt in shallow water for clams, mussels, fish, frogs, and crayfish.

Young raccoons discover that crayfish pinch. They soon learn to bite a crayfish head first, so it won't pinch them.

Raccoons find prey in water
by dabbling, or patting, the
stream bottom. Their tender
paws can tell them what is
there by instinct or by touch.

Raccoons live alone and spend most of their time hunting in their home range. This is an area that a raccoon claims as its own. A raccoon marks its claim by leaving its scent around the home range.

A yearling, or year-old, raccoon must look for an area where no other raccoons live. Then it leaves its scent there to claim it as a home range.

Raccoon tracks are often found along a stream. Minnow tails, crayfish claws, and toad skins may litter the path. These are left behind from raccoon meals.

Raccoons run from their enemies. They also climb trees or swim to escape. If cornered, a raccoon tries to scare away an attacker by raising the hair on its back and showing its teeth. It lowers its snout and growls. It can give off a bad smell to make enemies flee.

Wild raccoons can live up to twelve years. Great horned owls, eagles, and bobcats eat

young raccoons. Cougars, wolves, alligators, and coyotes eat adults.

In the autumn, raccoons eat great amounts of food to store up fat for the winter. Their fur also grows thick and shiny.

During winter, raccoons hibernate, or sleep, in their dens. They come out during warm spells.

In autumn, adult raccoons weigh between 20 to 30 pounds (9 to 14 kilograms). During winter, they live off their body fat. In spring, raccoons mate. The babies are born about six weeks later.

In earlier times, people wore raccoon fur and ate raccoon meat. They used the fat for cooking and as a salve. The people pictured know that raccoons belong in the wild.

Raccoons are not pets. They are wild animals that belong in their homes in nature.

When people destroy natural areas, raccoon ranges also disappear. This is a great loss because raccoons belong to the web of life. They help balance the numbers of other animals.

Raccoons are trying to adjust to all the changes humans have made to the environment.

It is up to us to see that raccoons' habitat is not destroyed so these animals have a chance to survive.

Glossary

burrow – a hole dug in the ground by an animal, often used as a home

dabbling – the way a raccoon pats shallow water searching for food

hibernate – to spend the winter in a resting state

home range – the area in which an animal stays for feeding, hunting, or denning

instinct – natural responses or ways of behaving

kits – young, fur-bearing animals, such as raccoons or foxes

mate – to join together to produce offspring

nocturnal – active mostly at night

web of life – the living things that are part of the environment that all have an effect on one another

yearling – an animal that is one year old

Index